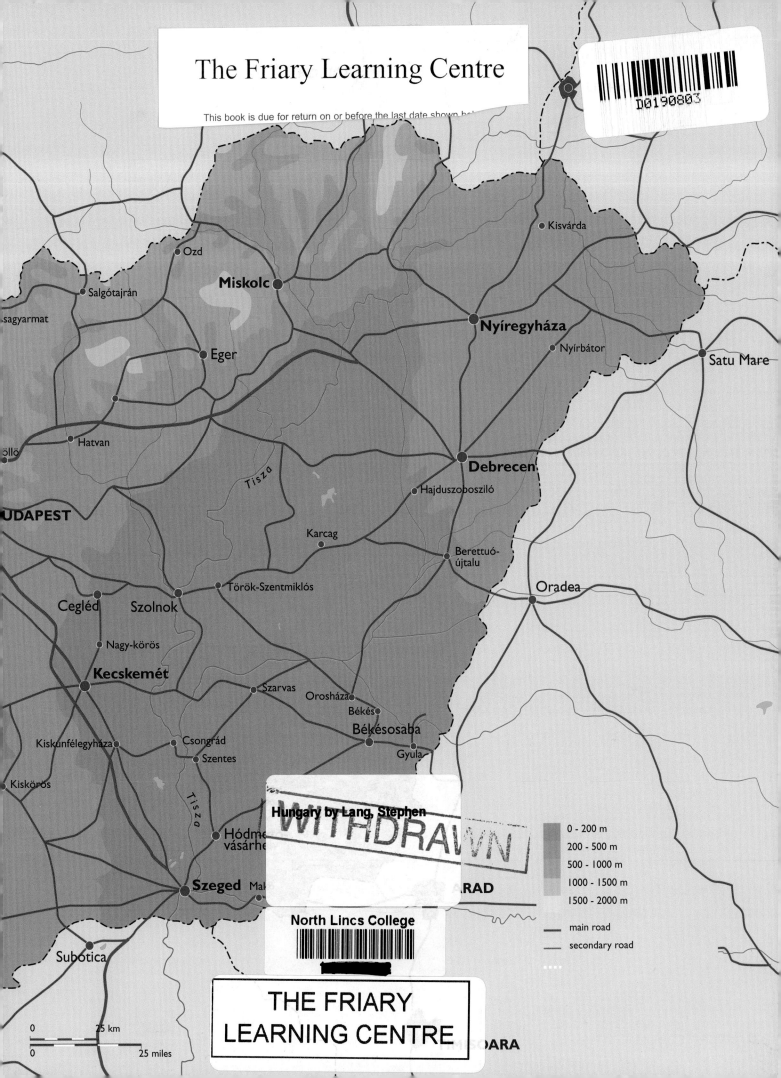

Kisvárda

Ozd

Miskolc

Salgótajrán

sagyarmat

Nyíregyháza

Nyírbátor

Satu Mare

Eger

öllö

Hatvan

Tisza

Debrecen

UDAPEST

Hajduszobosziló

Karcag

Berettuó-
újtalu

Oradea

Török-Szentmiklós

Cegléd

Szolnok

Nagy-körös

Kecskemét

Szarvas

Orosháza

Békés

Kiskunfélegyháza

Csongrád

Szentes

Békésosaba

Gyula

Kiskörös

Tisza

Hódme
vásárhe

RAD

Szeged Mak

	0 - 200 m
	200 - 500 m
	500 - 1000 m
	1000 - 1500 m
	1500 - 2000 m
	main road
	secondary road
.....	

Subotica

DARA

0   25 km

0   25 miles

New EU Countries and Citizens

Hungary

Stephan Lang

A Cherrytree Book

This edition published in 2006 by Evans Brothers Limited
2A Portman Mansions
Chiltern Street
London W1U 6NR, UK

Published by arrangement with KIT Publishers, The Netherlands

British Library Cataloguing-in-Publication Data
Lang, Stephan
Hungary. - (New EU countries and citizens)
1. Hungary - Juvenile literature
I. Title
943.9
ISBN 1842343246
9781842343241

Text: Stephan Lang
Photographs: Jan Willem Bultje
Translation: Wilma Hoving
UK editing: Sonya Newland
Design and Layout: Grafisch Ontwerpbureau Agaatsz BNO, Meppel, The Netherlands
Cover: Big Blu Ltd
Cartography: Armand Haye, Amsterdam, The Netherlands
Production: J & P Far East Productions, Soest, The Netherlands

Picture Credits
Photographs: Jan Willem Bultje
p.20 (top), 44 (bottom left) Peter Lehoczky, p. 44 (top right) Peter Orosz, p. 27, 37, 38, 44
(top left) Atilla Kisbenedek, p.39 Mario dudar: EPA Photo, p.22 (bottom), p.23 (top): Willy
Ebbens; p. 26 (top), 28 (bottom): EPA Photo; p. 36(t) © Paul Almasy/CORBIS; p. 45(b) ©
Yiorgos Nikiteas; Eye Ubiquitous/CORBIS; p. 46(r) © Reuters/CORBIS; p. 47 © BALAZS
GARDI/Reuters/CORBIS

Contents

Introduction

Hungary is situated in Central Europe, in an area called the Carpathian Basin. It is surrounded by mountains – the Carpathian Mountains in the north and east, and the Alps in the south and west.

Hungary is completely landlocked – it has no coastal boundaries. It is bordered to the north by Slovakia and the Ukraine, in the east by Romania, in the south by Croatia and Slovenia, and in the west by Austria. This situation has had a great effect on Hungary's history, resulting in significant changes to its boundaries over the centuries as other nations have invaded, conquered and divided the region. However, the area fell into the hands of the Hungarians' ancestors – the Magyar tribes – when they invaded and drove out the existing settlers.

For many years, the Kingdom of Hungary was vast and its rulers very powerful, but gradually they lost this power to other nations and by the middle of the twentieth century Hungarian territories were a fraction of what they had once been. The twentieth century was a particularly turbulent time for the Hungarian people, as they saw the loss of their homelands, and were forced to live under communist rule.

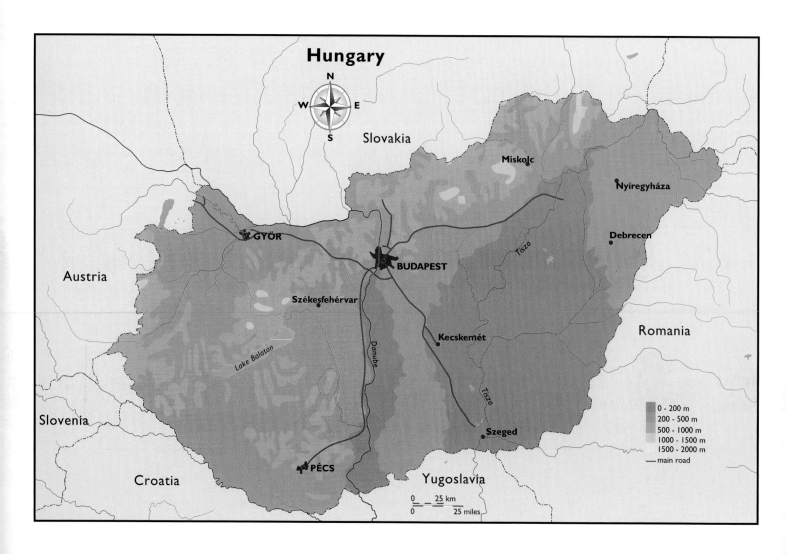

When the boundaries between Eastern and Western Europe began to fall in 1989, Hungary finally opened up to western influence. Today it is a parliamentary democracy, and enjoys good relations with its neighbouring countries. The economy is improving and its membership of international organisations such as NATO and the European Union have provided more stability for Hungary.

Its long history and ancient customs and traditions make Hungary a fascinating place to visit. It is a land of mountains and plains, rivers and lakes, and has a continental climate, making it very pleasant in the summer. The country's capital, Budapest, is now a popular tourist destination and is a thriving centre of Hungarian life and culture. Other areas are also attracting more visitors, who come to enjoy the country's architecture and carefully preserved natural beauty.

▲ *In some villages, particularly in the Puszta region of eastern Hungary, life has remained the same for centuries. Many people have only just received electricity and telephone lines.*

▼ *Hungary has some magnificent architecture, dating from several different periods. This is the town hall in Györ, built in the nineteenth century.*

History

Not much is known about who the original Hungarians were and where they came from before they settled in their present homeland, but archeological evidence has given us a few clues. We know that they were descended from a pagan tribe called the Magyars, which conquered the Carpathian Basin in the ninth century AD.

The Magyars have been traced back to the first century AD, to a region both east and west of the Ural Mountains, which lie on the border between Asia and Europe in present-day Russia. They were hunters and fishermen, and were excellent horsemen and archers. They lived a nomadic life, moving from place to place and sleeping in tents made of a wooden frame covered in animal hide, which could be easily transported. Gradually they migrated southwards along the Volga River, as far as the Black Sea.

At this time, the Carpathian Basin was a province of Rome, but the Romans had been driven out by the Huns, led by Attila. The body of the mighty Attila the Hun was buried in the bed of the Tisza River, which flows through eastern Hungary. By the time the Magyars reached the area, it was inhabited only by a sparse population of Slavs.

▼ *These statues commemorate Árpád – one of the first rulers of Hungary.*

The mighty Magyars

At the time of the conquest, the Magyars were organised in family clans, and these clans evolved to become great tribes with different languages. There were seven Magyar tribes and the strongest of these was the Megyer. The words *Magyar* (Hungarian) and *Magyarország* (Hungary), still used today, come from the language of the Megyer tribe.

The swift warriors of the Magyar tribes raided the whole of Europe, from the Byzantine Empire to the North Sea. These areas had already been plundered by the Vikings and the people living there were in constant fear of both the Vikings' swords and the Magyars' arrows.

▲ A statue of King Stephen, who was made a saint after converting his people to Christianity.

◄ King Stephen is an important figure in Hungarian history; this is a rock-opera about his life.

Early in the tenth century, the chieftain of one of these conquering tribes was Árpád. He was a great military leader, and his descendants became the hereditary chieftains. In this way Árpád founded the first Hungarian ruling dynasty.

It was not long, however, before the Magyars realised that they had to change their type of existence. After a crushing defeat in Bavaria in AD 955, the chieftain, Géza, decided that in order to survive and grow even stronger they must give up their nomadic way of life. Géza was the last pagan chieftain of the Magyars. His son, István, was raised as a Christian. According to legend, István was crowned as King Stephen on Christmas Day in the year 1000. The pope presented him with a royal crown. King Stephen was canonised in 1083 and as Saint Stephen he has been a figure of inspiration for the Hungarians for centuries. In the 1980s, during the communist era, a rock-opera about his life was staged.

▲ *Sultan Suleiman, who led the Turkish troops to victory at Mohács.*

Ottoman occupation

The next real threat to Hungarian territory came in the sixteenth century. By this time, the Ottoman (Turkish) Empire had grown very large and powerful, and the Turks posed a threat to the whole of Europe.

In August 1526, the Turkish sultan Suleiman and 80,000 heavily armed soldiers besieged the city of Mohács in the south of Hungary. The Hungarian army could not defend the city against such an attack – they only had 20,000 men, and they were poorly organised and badly equipped. The Battle of Mohács took place on 29 August and the sultan's army inflicted a crushing defeat on the Hungarians. The Hungarian king, Louis (Lajos), who was barely 20 years old, was killed in the battle. The Ottoman occupation of a large part of Hungary lasted more than 150 years.

Habsburg rule

King Louis' young widow, Mary of Hungary, was a Habsburg, and because of this the Hapsburgs claimed Hungary as part of their empire when the king died. Mary's brother, Ferdinand, was crowned king of Hungary and the country became part of the Habsburg Empire, alongside Germany, the Netherlands, Spain and Austria. Mary's other brother, Emperor Charles V, later made her governor of the Netherlands. She chose the city of Brussels in present-day Belgium as her residence. However, even from there she kept trying to remove the Turks from her former kingdom in Hungary.

However, in the east of the country, a group of nobles resented being ruled by a foreigner, and so they elected a man named John Zapolya as their king.

During the Turkish occupation, therefore, Hungary was split into three parts. The Turks had control of central and southern Hungary; the Austrian Habsburg dynasty controlled Royal Hungary, which consisted of counties along the Austrian border and a part of north-western Croatia; and Transylvania (located in present-day Romania) was ruled by the nobles in the east.

During the period of Ottoman occupation, the Reformation (a religious reaction against corruption in the Catholic Church) began to sweep through Europe. The Habsburgs were Catholics. In Transylvania, the nobility and lower classes embraced forms of the new Protestant religion. The Transylvanian rulers even joined forces with the Turks.

▲ *Mary of Hungary was part of the Austrian Habsburg dynasty, and when her husband, King Louis of Hungary, was killed by the Turks, her family claimed Hungary as part of its empire.*

At the end of the seventeenth century the Habsburgs finally succeeded in driving the Turks out of Hungary, and the whole country became part of the Habsburg Empire. However, the Habsburgs met with great resistance among the people. *Betyár* (outlaws) and Protestants who were forced to hide out in swamps and woods fought against what they saw as Catholic oppression. The most famous of these outlaws was Sándor Rózsa, who became a national hero. In the end, however, even he was tracked down and executed.

The Hungarian Revolution

In 1848, many revolutions broke out in European countries, including Hungary. The revolt started on 15 March, with a proclamation and demonstrations against the monarchy. The people were led by Hungary's most renowned poet, Sándor Petöfi, and Lajos Kossuth was elected governor-president of the people.

It was a violent revolution but eventually, with the help of Russian troops, the Habsburgs managed to suppress the people. Sándor Petöfi fell in battle at Pisjki (in present-day Romania), and Lajos Kossuth was forced into exile.

After the revolution, difficult negotiations finally resulted in a compromise between the Habsburgs and Hungarians. Emperor Franz Josef was made king of Hungary, largely due to the popularity of his wife Elisabeth (known as Sisi), who loved the Hungarians. This became known as the 'Dual Monarchy of Austria-Hungary', or the 'Danube Monarchy'. Hungary was granted its own government and some authority over its domestic affairs. At the end of the century, a parliament house was built in Budapest. This marked the beginning of a time of prosperity for Hungary, which lasted until the end of the First World War in 1918.

▲ *This plaque commemorates Lajos Kossuth, governor of Hungary in 1849.*

▼ *Budapest became the seat of Hungarian rule in the nineteenth century.*

The First World War

In June 1914, a Bosnian Serb assassinated the heir to the Austrian throne, starting a conflict between the two countries that would quickly draw in many other European countries and escalate into the First World War. Hungarian soldiers fought in trenches on the Eastern Front near Galicia in Poland.

In 1917, the Bolshevik Revolution took place in Russia, overthrowing the monarchy and establishing a communist government. By the end of the war, several European states, including Czechoslovakia and Poland, were demanding their independence. Hungary also wanted to be an independent country, and for the first time this seemed to be a real possibility. The Habsburg Empire had effectively collapsed after being on the losing side of the war.

A communist government under the influence of Soviet Russia was established in Hungary: the Hungarian Soviet Republic ruled for only 100 days. This period was known as the 'Red Terror'. The communist leaders travelled throughout the country, executing many innocent people.

▲ *The coats of arms of the different lands that were part of the Austro-Hungarian Empire.*

The Treaty of Trianon

After 100 days, the communist leaders were overthrown and they all fled abroad. The Hungarian Red Army was defeated by the Romanian army. Supported by France, Romanian forces occupied Transylvania and the land east of the River Danube, including Hungary's capital, Budapest.

In 1920, the leaders of France, Britain and the United States – the allies who had won the war – divided Hungarian lands amongst themselves. Hungary's signing of the Treaty of Trianon at Versailles, near Paris, lost the country two-thirds of its territory, containing more than one-third of its population. New states were established – including Czechoslovakia and Yugoslavia.

▶ *This photograph, taken on 1 May 1919, shows a procession of people marching to work in Hungary, during the time of the communist regime.*

The Hungarian monarchy was restored, but the ruling body decided not to recall the Hungarian king, Charles IV, who was in exile. Instead, Commander Miklós Horthy was elected to serve as regent. In the years leading up to the Second World War (1939–45), Horthy began to support the German leader Adolf Hitler, because he was reclaiming land that had been taken away after the First World War, and Horthy hoped to regain some former Hungarian territories. When the tide began to turn against Germany in 1944, Horthy started to negotiate with his former enemy, Soviet Russia, but he was overthrown later that year.

▲ *Admiral Miklós Horthy, who ruled Hungary from 1920 to 1944.*

Communism

In the spring of 1945, Germany was defeated. Europe split into two parts: the free West and the countries in the East, which came under Soviet communist influence. A boundary nicknamed the 'Iron Curtain' ran through Europe from the North Sea to the Black Sea. Hungary became one of the Warsaw Pact countries in the East.

The Russians banned democratic political parties, and the population was oppressed by the Communist Party. Businesses were not allowed to be privately owned, and farmers were forced to part with their lands and instead had to work on communal land known as co-operatives.

The oppressed Hungarians revolted in 1956. The West encouraged the revolution, but when Russian tanks rolled into the country, states in the West offered no help, and the Russians put down the revolution with much bloodshed.

Independence

The communist regime lasted more than 40 years. In 1989, leaders of several eastern bloc countries started working towards reunification with the West. This led to the fall of the Berlin Wall in Germany, and eventually to the fall of communism.

Hungary has since been a free, democratic country, with an elected parliament and elected leaders.

◄ *The Hungarian flag flying on the Chain Bridge in Budapest, alongside the flag of the European Union, which the country joined on 1 May 2004.*

The country

Hungary is situated in central Europe. Its territory extends over 93,030 square kilometres, and it measures 528 km from east to west and 319 km from north to south.

Hungary is surrounded by land and has some 2,171 km of borders. It is 400 km from the Mediterranean Sea, 800 km from the Baltic Sea and the Black Sea, and 1,200 km from the Atlantic Ocean.

Geographic regions

Hungary has three main geographic regions: Tiszántúl, the territory east of the Tisza River; Duna-Tiszaköze, the land between the Danube and Tisza Rivers in central Hungary; and Transdanubia or Dunántúl, the area west of the Danube. These regions are divided into a number of districts.

▲ *The Tisza River marks the boundary between the Tiszántúl and Duna-Tiszaköze regions.*

The Northern Hills lie in the north, bordering on Slovakia. Among these hills are the Matra Mountains, containing Hungary's highest peak, Kékes (1,014 metres). In eastern Hungary lies the Great Plain. It has a variety of terrains, among which is the renowned Puszta, a vast area of grassland. West of the Danube lie the Transdanubian Central Mountains. South of Lake Balaton are the Transdanubian Hills and in the north lie the foothills of the Carpathian Mountains. In the west are the foothills of the Alps.

▶ *The Puszta in the eastern part of Hungary was once covered with rich soil. Today the land is dry and little of it can be used for agriculture. Cattle and sheep now graze on this area of grassland.*

Rivers and Lakes

The River Danube runs through the middle of Hungary. It is the second-longest European river (the Volga is the longest), and the most important river in Central Europe. The Danube is 2,860 km long, 417 km of which flow through Hungary. The river enters the country in the north-west, where it serves as the border with Slovakia for a stretch of 140 km. The river leaves the country in the south, near the city of Mohács. Four European capitals are situated on the Danube: Vienna in Austria, Bratislava in Slovakia, Budapest in Hungary, and Belgrade in Serbia-Montenegro.

The second most important river is the Tisza, of which 596 km run through Hungary. The Tisza River flows through the Great Plains region in the east of the country. It rises in the Carpathian Mountains, in Romania, and flows into the River Danube in present-day Serbia-Montenegro.

Hungary's third major river is the Dráva, which forms part of the border with Croatia in the south. The Dráva River also flows into the Danube.

Lake Balaton is Hungary's most important lake and is the largest in Central Europe. It is one of Hungary's major tourist resorts. Lake Balaton is 72 km long and varies in width from 1.5 km to 11 km at various points. Its total surface area amounts to 597 square km.

▲ *Margit Island in the River Danube.*

Caves

Hungary has over 3,000 caves. The Aggtelek National Park has one of the most extensive cave systems in Europe. Most of the Aggtelek cave system is located within Hungary, but about nine of its 26 kilometres stretch into Slovakia. The rock is very soft, and rainwater easily seeps through it. This causes erosion, creating caves and underground streams. Calcifying rainwater has formed stalactites, occasionally in odd shapes and colours. Traces of prehistoric man have been found in these caves.

Other caves can be found in the capital Budapest. Palvölgy is the largest stalagmite cave, with underground passages stretching out for 13 km. The cave has been formed by thermal springs, and lies 82 metres deep. The acoustics of the cave are exceptionally good, and concerts are performed there regularly.

▶ *Within the Aggtelek caves there are hundreds of stalagtites, formed over many centuries.*

▲ *The summer months are hot in Hungary.*

▲ *Winters can be quite severe.*

Climate

Hungary enjoys a temperate climate. It is influenced by three main climatic areas: Atlantic, continental and Mediterranean. The weather is affected by cold air streams from the north, and humid, cool air-streams from the Atlantic Ocean. Warm air-streams originate in the Mediterranean and from Eastern Europe. Consequently, Hungary has a continental climate with long, cold winters and hot summers.

The average annual temperature is 9.7°C. In summer, temperatures can rise to between 35 and 40°C; in winter, temperatures may fall as low as 25 to 30 degrees below zero.

▼ *High levels of rainfall can cause the water level in rivers and lakes to rise dramatically, and this can lead to flooding.*

Compared to other European countries, Hungary has the greatest number of hours of sun, averaging between 1,700 and 2,200 hours every year. The area that enjoys the most sunlight lies between the Danube and Tisza Rivers; the area with the least sun lies at the foot of the Alps in the west of Hungary. Summer brings long dry periods, and autumn and spring bring an abundance of rainfall. During these times, storms accompanied by high winds can cause damage to crops.

Towns and cities

There are several large cities in Hungary – the capital Budapest is the largest. Several of these cities have grown up over many centuries and in some areas the settlements date back to Roman times. The towns and cities are bustling centres of modern life, with all that other major European cities have to offer.

Villages

Despite this, Hungary is really a rural country, and there are more than 3,000 small villages scattered across the landscape. Many of these are very old and have sites of historical interest. In the mountains of northern Hungary lies the tiny village of Holloko, which contains buildings in the seventeenth-century folk architecture style, and which is now on UNESCO's World Heritage list.

There are also many hamlets in the Puszta region, which often have only a handful of houses. People have lived in relative isolation for centuries, and only recently have they had electricity, telephone lines – and even roads.

▲ *A sign welcomes visitors to the small village of Melykút.*

Budapest

Budapest is actually made up of two parts that were once towns in their own right: Buda and Pest. Buda is situated on the right bank of the River Danube. This is the oldest part of the city and it was once the capital of the kingdom of Hungary. In the first century AD there was a Roman settlement here: Aquincumin. Now the area is protected as an ancient monument. On a hill rising high above the river lies the Royal Castle, near the thirteenth-century Matthias Church.

Buda is the fashionable part of the city, and on the slopes of the hills lie the shaded residential areas where the wealthy live.

◀ *The Chain Bridge in Budapest, with Buda on the near side and Pest across the river.*

Across the river lies Pest. Here there are crowded shopping-streets, wide boulevards, restaurants, coffee-houses, and the magnificent hotels dating from the golden era, when Budapest was the capital of the kingdom of Hungary and part of the Habsburg Empire. At that time Hungary was twice its present size in area. Nowadays, with nearly two million inhabitants, Budapest has trouble accommodating all the people in the city. About one in every five Hungarians resides in the capital.

The Chain Bridge was the first physical link across the water between Buda and Pest. It was designed by the English engineer Adam Clark, and built between 1839 and 1849. From this time, the two cities became one, although this was not official until 1862. Large parts of the city have been damaged and rebuilt over the centuries, and it was occupied by the Turks for more than 100 years. By the time the Russians recaptured the city from the Germans in 1945, all bridges were destroyed and many buildings had been ruined.

The crown jewels, including the crown that Pope Sylvester II presented to King Stephen in the year 1000, are kept in the parliament building in Budapest. At the end of the Second World War American soldiers took the crown home with them and it was not returned until 1976. Even though Hungary is a republic today, the crown is still depicted on the national coat of arms.

▼ *The Chain Bridge is guarded at each end by stone lions.*

▲ *People enjoying the atmosphere in one of Hungary's old coffee-houses.*

Coffee-Houses

There are few countries that can boast as many beautiful old coffee-houses as Hungary. Budapest alone has nearly 200. The most famous example is Gerbaud, in Vörösmarty Square. The original owner, after whom the coffee-house is named, was the inventor of a special kind of pastry that is still served in the coffee-house.

Debrecen

In the middle of the Puszta region lies the second-largest city in Hungary: Debrecen. Compared with Budapest, which is almost ten times bigger, Debrecen is a quiet provincial town. It is an old university town that had strong relations with the Netherlands in the seventeenth century. At the rear of the large Reformed Church temple stands the Galley-slave Column. During the period of Catholic Restoration under the Habsburgs, 733 Protestant preachers and teachers stood trial here. Forty of them were transported to Naples as galley-slaves. Protestant cities such as Geneva and Zurich collected money to free them.

▶ *A floral parade through the steets of Debrecen.*

Pecs

The city of Pecs lies close to the Croatian border and is a truly southern city, with a Mediterranean climate. It is an important university city – the oldest Hungarian university was founded there in 1367. Pecs was occupied by the Turks for many years and the Ottoman influence is still noticeable all over the city. The Mosque of Pasha Gazi Khassim, which is now a Roman Catholic church, is the most famous example of Turkish architecture in the country.

▶ *The Djzami Mosque in Pecs is evidence of the Muslim Turks' presence in Hungary.*

People and culture

Hungary's population numbers around 10 million. However, many Hungarians live outside Hungary. In virtually all neighbouring countries, including Serbia-Montenegro, Austria, Croatia and Slovakia, large Hungarian communities can be found. The largest of these – two million people – can be found in Transylvania, in Romania.

Within Hungary, nearly 90 per cent of the population is Hungarian. The largest minority group is the Roma, or gypsies (around 4 per cent). Roma have lived in Central Europe for centuries and they have endured much discrimination in the past. The majority of the Roma speak or understand Hungarian, but many also speak their own language, Romanes. A number of Roma lead a nomadic existence, but others have enjoyed a good education or make a contribution to Hungarian culture, as musicians, for example. Other ethnic groups include Germans, Serbs, Slovaks and Romanians.

Language

The Hungarian language differs from that of its neighbouring countries. These belong to the family of Indo-European languages. Hungarian, however, belongs to a language family known as Finno-Ugric, and is related to Finnish, Estonian, Komi (from north-eastern Russia), and languages spoken in parts of the Ural Mountain region. It has been intermingled with Turkish, Slavic, German, Latin and French words. There are various dialects spoken throughout the country. Hungarian is written using the traditional Latin alphabet, with a few diactric marks (accents).

Hungarian is the only official national language, but during Habsburg rule, many Hungarians spoke German as well. The Jewish community, which was extensive before the Second World War, especially in the cities, spoke its own language, Yiddish. The Holocaust decimated the Jewish community. Of the 900,000 Hungarian Jews, only one-third survived the war. Many of these emigrated to Israel. Today, however, many Jewish Hungarians are returning to their native country.

Religion

Today, the majority of Hungarians are Roman Catholics (approximately 70 per cent), with around 25 per cent following various Protestant offshoots. However, in the seventeenth century nearly 90 per cent of the population was Protestant. During the Counter-Reformation, Roman Catholicism grew in popularity.

◀ *The Eger Cathedral, in Eger, north-eastern Hungary, shows the Turkish influence.*

Hadasa and Eszter from Israel pose for a photograph by the Budapest Synagogue. Their grandparents came from Hungary and survived the Holocaust. After the Second World War they emigrated to Israel. Hadasa and Eszter still speak good Hungarian and are here researching their family tree. They visited the Holocaust Museum that has recently opened in Budapest. The museum is the only one of its kind in Eastern Europe.

▼ *The library in the Benedictine Abbey in Pannonhalma. The abbey was established in AD 996, and the monks here wrote the first manuscripts in the Hungarian language in 1055.*

During the period of the communist regime (1948–89), the Churches were persecuted and oppressed. Teachers were strictly forbidden to attend church services. Members of the Communist Party were not allowed to be buried with a Christian cross, only with a red star.

There are hundreds of Roman Catholic churches and monasteries across Hungary. There are also Protestant churches, Jewish synagogues, and even mosques dating from the period of Muslim Turkish rule.

In a separate chapel within the Budapest Basilica is a reliquary containing the right hand of King Stephen, the first Christian king of Hungary, who was later canonised.

Stephen's coronation in the year 1000 took place in the old capital, Esztergom, situated at the confluence of the Thron and Danube rivers. Esztergom was the first residence of the Hungarian kings and the archbishop of Hungary still has his seat there. In 1242, Esztergom was destroyed by raiding Mongols. The largest church in Hungary was built in Esztergom in the nineteenth century, on the site of the eleventh-century cathedral. The enormous basilica, modelled after Saint Peter's in Rome, is set on a hill above the city, and its gigantic dome measures 72 metres.

◄ *The enormous church, modelled on St Peter's basilica in Rome, was built in Esztergom in the nineteenth century.*

Celebrations and festivals

Hungarians celebrate their 'name day' rather than their birthday. The name day is the day that is devoted to the saint after whom a person is named. For example, all Sándors (after Sándor Csoma Kôrösi, who lived 1784–1842) celebrate their name day on 18 March, all Jozsefs (Joseph) on 19 March, and all Benedeks (Benedict) on 20 March. According to an old rhyme, Sándor, Jozsef and Benedek bring along the warm weather in their bags. These three saints' days announce the beginning of spring.

On 6 December, Hungarian children receive a visit from Mikulas (Saint Nicholas), who wears bishop's robes and a red mitre on his head; he carries a staff in one hand and a sack of small gifts in the other. He is accompanied by a boy in a black costume, equipped with horns and a tail. The boy carries a switch made of dry twigs with which to smack any naughty children. Each child receives a small present – usually a toy or sweets – from Mikulas.

▲▼ 'Csárdás' are danced at celebrations. This traditional Hungarian dance starts off very slowly and gradually picks up speed. The dancers wear traditional costumes, including a wide skirt (usually red) for the women.

▼ Masked figures are believed to chase away the winter.

Gypsy weddings are renowned, with wild, stirring music, where the 'gadzos' (non-Romas) are equally welcome. Hungarian weddings, even in the cities, still have a very traditional feel to them, with music and dancing. The csárdás, Hungary's national dance, starts off slow, easy and sedate, but ends up at a fast, whirling pace.

Every year, each village celebrates the feast of its patron saint, the *bucsu*. Friends and relatives come from far and wide to the village. A fair is held and the feast traditionally closes with the village ball.

In the village of Janoshida, in Transylvania (Romania), where there is a large Hungarian community, they still observe Hungarian customs and traditions. An annual 'maiden market' takes place where girls are symbolically 'sold'. Traditionally, young men who were planning to get married would come from far-away villages with their horses and ox-carts to find a wife. Both men and women wear the traditional dress.

▲ *These schoolchildren are taking part in the* bucsu *festival, in which villages honour their patron saints.*

Busójárás is among the most unusual feasts in Hungary. The tradition dates back to 1526, when the Battle of Mohács took place in which the Hungarian army was defeated by the Turks (see page 8). The feast has developed into a merry, carnivalesque event, attracting tens of thousands of tourists every year. Figures wearing sheepskins and terrifying masks walk through the streets, and children shake bags filled with sawdust and feathers, and make loud banging noises, while a medieval cannon is carried along in the procession. When dusk falls, a large fire is lit in the central square, to symbolically burn the winter, in the form of a straw doll.

Thermal baths

The qualities of Hungarian thermal water were first recognised by the Romans. The bath culture reached its peak during the Turkish occupation and some bath-houses from that period are still in use. Hungary has more than 1,000 medicinal spas. Their curative effect is brought about both by drinking the water and bathing in it. The water of Héviz Lake, not far from Lake Balaton, has a constant temperature of 33°C. Tapoica, in the north-east, is Europe's only medicinal spa inside a cave.

◄ *Excavations on a Roman bath-house in Pecs.*

◀ ▲ *The Central Market-Hall in Budapest draws locals and tourists alike to enjoy the fresh produce available there.*

Markets

Hungary has many market-halls. The largest and best known is the Central Market-Hall in Budapest, built in the late nineteenth century by Samu Pecz. It had grown very run-down, but it has recently been restored to its original style.

While many markets in the cities are covered, just about every town and village has its own open-air market. These are often open weekly, and farmers come from miles around to trade their products, such as live poultry, pigs, cattle and corn.

After the collapse of the communist regime in 1989, black markets were set up in the east, where traders from Moldavia, the Ukraine and Romania offered many different products, such as fake designer clothing and kitchen appliances, as well as illegal electronics, software and CDs.

◀ *The black market in Nyíregyháza. This and others like it are often filled with illegal products.*

Barnoesj and Zsezsó are at the black market in Nyíregyháza with their father and grandfather. Their father wants to buy inexpensive tyres for his car and cheap petrol, smuggled out of the Ukraine and Romania. Barnoesj is interested in buying computer games. Zsezsó wants clothes and shoes. Afterwards, their grandfather treats Barnoesj and Zsezsó to an ice-cream. Cheap electrical goods, CDs, watches and even car parts are usually available at the black markets.

Black (or 'smuggling') markets are nicknamed 'Comecon Markets' by the Hungarian people, after the former economic block led by the Soviet Union. Petrol smuggling from Romania and especially the Ukraine has been very profitable in these regions, and provides many inhabitants with extra income which is much needed. These markets are popular, because the goods are much cheaper than in shops or legal markets, but it is hoped that they will slowly disappear now that Hungary has joined the European Union and introduced visa requirements.

Shops

▼ *Large supermarkets began to open in Hungary after the free-market economy was established.*

During the communist era only state-run shops existed. The economy was centrally planned, which meant that the retail trade was under strict supervision. After 1989, a free-market economy was set up and private shops have opened throughout the country. The free-market economy also saw the arrival of large supermarkets – often joint ventures between foreign companies and local enterprises. In Budapest, and in the other larger cities, chic shopping streets have appeared, selling all the top international brands. However, for most Hungarians these articles remain too expensive to buy.

Music

Hungary is renowned for its gypsy and folk music, and a number of famous composers were Hungarian by birth.

Franz Liszt (1811–86) is perhaps Hungary's most famous composer. He not only wrote music but was a renowned pianist, and his work represents the high point of the nineteenth-century Romantic movement in music. Among his best-loved pieces are the *Hungarian Rhapsodies.*

Béla Bartók (1881–1945) not only composed operas, such as *Bluebeard's Castle,* but also collected many traditional Hungarian folk melodies, and incorporated them into his compositions. He disagreed with the Nazi laws established in Hungary during the Second World War, and so he emigrated to the USA.

The composer Josef Haydn (1732–1809) was inspired by Hungarian culture. Born in Vienna, in Austria, Haydn was offered a job with the wealthy and influential family of Hungarian nobles, the Eszterházys. In summer, concerts are still performed at Eszterházy Castle.

▲ *Béla Bartók (top) was passionately patriotic, and stood up against German occupation of his country during the Second World War.*

Like Bartók, Zoltán Kodály (1882–1967) composed music with a strong Hungarian influence, although his music was less radical than Bartók's. He spent time travelling around his native country collecting traditional folksongs, and worked these into his compositions. His most famous works include the *Peacock Variations,* based on a Hungarian folk tune, and several Hungarian dances. He was also very influential in music education and wrote several pieces to help children learn music.

▲ *Franz Liszt was born in Raiding (then in Hungary, now part of Austria). His piano performances drew vast crowds and he toured all over Europe.*

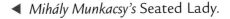
◀ *Mihály Munkacsy's* Seated Lady.

Art

Hungary has produced some important painters. Mihály Munkácsy (1844–1900) painted many realistic scenes from life as well as several landscapes. Among his most famous works is a piece called *Hungarian Conquest*, which he painted for the Houses of Parliament.

Tivadar Csontváry's (1912–89) paintings won international acclaim. Among his most famous works are *The Solitary Cedar* and *View of the Dead Sea from the Temple Square in Jerusalem*.

National Song

Rise up, Magyar, the country calls!
It's 'now or never' what fate befalls...
Shall we live as slaves or free men?
That's the question — choose your
  'Amen'!
God of Hungarians,
We swear unto Thee,
We swear unto Thee — that slaves
  We shall
No longer be!

Sándor Petöfi

Literature

Numerous poets are revered in Hungary and Hungarian poets have often inspired the nation and encouraged the people in their resistance against oppression. According to legend, the 1848 Revolution against the Habsburgs (see page 9) started with the poem *National Song*, by Sándor Petöfi.

After the War of Independence, the realistic novel became fashionable. This was the era of Zsigmond Kemény and Mór Jókai. Contemporary Hungarian prose has gained international acclaim and Imre Kértész received the Nobel Prize for Literature in 2002.

▼ *Imre Kértész's novel* Liquidation, *set in Budapest in the 1980s.*

Media

Before 1989, all media fell under control of the communist state. There was state television and state radio, there were state publishing companies and state newspapers. There was no freedom of the press or the media. Books by many well-known authors could only be sold illegally and copies were smuggled in from abroad, for example, through the Hungarian community in what was then Yugoslavia. Illegal copies of banned books were called *samizdat*.

Since the fall of Communism, the media has opened up again. A great number of commercial stations are in operation, besides public radio and television channels. The printed media, such as newspapers, books and magazines, is also flourishing.

Government

Since October 1989, the Republic of Hungary has been a parliamentary democracy with a multi-party system. There are 19 administrative divisions, or counties, in Hungary. The Executive branch of the government is run by the prime minister and a council of ministers. The prime minister and his council are elected by the National Assembly on the recommendation of the president. Presidential elections are held every five years. All men and women over the age of 18 are allowed to vote. The president is the head of state, but his role and function are purely formal, and the country is run by the parliament.

▲ *Hungary's magnificent parliament buildings sit on the banks of the River Danube in Budapest.*

The main political parties are the Alliance of Free Democrats (SzDSz), the Hungarian Civic Alliance (Fidesz-MPP), the Hungarian Democratic People's Party (MDNP), the Hungarian Socialist Party (MSzP), and the Hungarian Workers' Party (MMP).

Although a Hungarian constitution has existed since 1949, this has been revised over the years. In 1989 the Constitution was amended to ensure legal rights for all individuals and to limit the authority of the prime minister. In 1997 the judicial system was improved through further constitutional changes. The rules of the legal system are based on those in Western Europe.

◀ *The parliamentary chamber in the Houses of Parliament in Budapest.*

Education

Education in Hungary suffered under the communist regime. Children were forced to study the Russian language, and learnt about Communism instead of gaining a broad education in more academic subjects. Since 1989, however, the system has been reformed and is now similar to that in other European countries.

Schooling in Hungary is compulsory between the ages of six and 18, although some children go to nursery school from the age of three. When they reach six they go to primary school. This is divided into two stages, each lasting four years. During the first four years children are taught by one class teacher, but in the second half of primary education they have different teachers specialising in different subjects. Among these are foreign languages, which are considered important in Hungary. Usually, English or German is offered at primary-school level.

Secondary schools

There are several types of secondary, or high schools that children can choose from. General secondary schools (gymnasiums), offer general education in a range of subjects and are intended to prepare children for university. Vocational secondary schools focus on specific subjects, training students for a particular profession. There are also technical schools for pupils who do not wish to continue their education after the age of 18.

There are a large number of Roma children in Hungary, and teaching programmes have been developed to help in their education. Special facilities have also been designed for children from other minority groups, such as Slovaks and Romanians.

It is not always possible to educate Hungarians who live in neighbouring countries in their native language, and they often have to learn the language of the country in which they are living.

▶ *Children spend eight years at primary, or elementary, school in Hungary.*

The Hungarian passion for mathematics is evident in the Rubik's Cube. This was designed by the Hungarian Ernö Rubik in 1974. Each side of the cube has nine moveable squares in different colours, and the aim is to cover each side with a single colour. It started a huge trend for this kind of puzzle in the 1980s and sold millions worldwide.

Higher education

At the end of secondary school, students take exams, and if they pass they can apply for a place at one of the universities. Here they can take undergraduate or postgraduate degrees and even go on to take doctoral degrees. There are a number of institutions for higher education in Hungary, including colleges for specialist training in technical subjects, medicine and sciences.

Education in the natural sciences is particularly popular and advanced in Hungary. Several scientists who have won the Nobel Prize for Physics or Chemistry are Hungarian, including John Polányi and John Harsányi.

Hungarian medical scientists and researchers have also contributed important work in the medical field.

▶ *The University of Debrecen in eastern Hungary was formally established in 2000, but it has its roots in the Reformed College of Debrecen, which was founded in 1538.*

▲ *The composer Zoltán Kodály was extremely influential in establishing methods of educating children in music. The bottom sign explains that the Zoltán Kodály institute used to be a Franciscan monastery and is now a national monument ('müemlék').*

▼ *The Zoltán Kodály institute is one of the most famous music schools in Hungary.*

Traditionally, music education is important in Hungary. The composer Zoltán Kodály (see page 24) believed that all children could be taught music by singing in choirs, and his methods are still used today. In the city of Kecskemét, where he lived and worked, advanced courses are offered to musicians and music teachers each year.

Science

The Hungarian interest in science is also evident through the many inventions they have come up with and discoveries they have made over the centuries.

The Hungarians were the first to discover that gold ore and silver ore could be separated by means of saltpetre. They were also the first to discover that gunpowder was not only useful in guns and cannons, but could also be used to blow up rocks, for example, to widen rivers and make it easier to navigate them.

Hungarian inventions range from an improved wheel suspension by the wheelwrights of the village of Kocs (the name of which is borrowed in many western languages to describe a vehicle with wheels: 'coach', 'Kutze', 'coche', 'koets'), to the ballpoint pen by Lászlo Biró and Andor Goy in 1939.

Cuisine

Hungarians love food and Hungary is known for its rich, spicy cuisine. Traditional dishes are cooked all year round, as well as on special occasions and during festivals.

▼ Contestants at Baja's annual fish-soup making competition.

Meat

Various types of meat are used in Hungarian cooking, but beef, pork and chicken are the most popular. The Mangalica pig and the grey long-horned cattle are unique to Hungary. Game meats are also used in Hungarian dishes. Roast goose is a common meal and duck, venison and wild boar can also be found on restaurant menus. Goulash is probably the best-known Hungarian dish, but there are many others, including paprika chicken and cabbage stuffed with minced beef. Many dishes are flavoured with onions, garlic and peppers and are hearty and full of flavour. Most main meals are accompanied by potatoes (potatoes often appear in Hungarian stews and other dishes), but both rice and pasta are also used.

Fish

Freshwater fish is popular in Hungary, and fish soup is another national dish. The recipes from Szeged and Baja are famous. The annual fish-soup contest in Baja attracts thousands of visitors and tourists each year in July. About 2,000 contestants simmer their delicious fish soup in large pots along the banks of the Danube. In Budapest, carp in batter is the traditional dish served on Christmas Eve.

◄ Peppers on a market stall. Both green and red peppers are used a lot in Hungarian dishes. Paprika is a seasoning made from sweet red peppers.

Pörkölt (goulash)

Paprika is very popular in Hungarian dishes, and apparently it was first used by Hungarian chefs. Paprika is essential to goulash (pörkölt), a stew with beef, pork or mutton in a spicy paprika sauce. Initially, this was an easy dish for travelling herdsmen to prepare in a pot hanging from a tripod over a wood fire. In the nineteenth century, goulash started to appear on the menus of the more exclusive restaurants, and the dish has now become something of a national symbol.

Desserts

Hungarians also love desserts. They enjoy sweet dishes such as pancakes filled with different jams or cream and nuts, and cakes, including dobos torta, a sponge-cake layered with chocolate and glazed with caramel and nuts. One of their favourite desserts is strudel, a light pastry with fillings such as apples or cherries. One of the more unusual desserts in Hungary is túró csusza – noodles served with cottage cheese, which is an ingredient used in several sweet dishes in Hungary.

Recipe for pörkölt

Ingredients
1 kilo leg of beef
2-3 onions
2-3 garlic cloves
2-3 fresh peppers
1-2 tomatoes
3 tablespoons lard or oil
Bay leaves
Whole peppercorns
Paprika
Caraway seeds
Salt

Cut the beef from the bone with into 2-cm cubes. Chop two or three onions and fry them in oil until they are transparent. Add the cubes of beef. Add tomatoes, peppers and garlic to taste. Season with salt, add one or two bay leaves, a few peppercorns and a pinch of ground caraway seed, if desired. Turn the heat down and simmer the stew. When the meat is half-cooked, sprinkle the dish lavishly with paprika. Simmer the stew without stirring in a pan with a lid on it. Remove the lid when the meat is tender, and simmer the stew until the sauce has reduced.

▲ *During the Décs grape festival, everyone celebrates the end of the grape harvest. These women are wearing the traditional clothes of central and south-western Hungary.*

Slaughter Feast

At the beginning of winter, in the weeks prior to the festive season, every farmer slaughters a pig. The Slaughter Feast (*Disznótor*) has its origins in the ancient pagan rituals of the Magyars. The farmer slaughters the pig in the morning, before sunrise, and it is roasted whole on a large straw fire. While the pig is roasting, the guests toast with Pálinka, an alcoholic fruit-based drink. Next, the carcass is washed and divided into chunks. Bacon and hams are pickled at first, and smoked a few weeks later. At night, neighbours and relatives visit to enjoy the feast, which lasts deep into the night. Hungarian children look forward to this feast for months.

Wine

Hungary is a well-known wine-making country, and vineyards can be found all across western and central regions of the country. It is therefore not surprising that wine is a popular drink all over Hungary. The favourite is the Tokaji wine, named after the village in the north of the country where it is made. Tokaji is a sweet wine and usually accompanies desserts.

▼ *The Villány wine-making region lies in the south-west, near the border with Croatia.*

Restaurants

Hungary has an extensive and highly developed restaurant culture, and the average person in Hungary eats out at least once a month. They do this not only to enjoy the food, but also to take in the festive atmosphere that can be found in most Hungarian restaurants. A typical Hungarian restaurant often has live music, provided by a gypsy or salon orchestra. Through the ages, the Roma have played an important part in the development of Hungarian musical culture.

The main cities, especially Budapest, have many fine restaurants, where it is possible to try all sorts of traditional cuisine. Among the best known are Gundel's and Matyas Kelder, which has a gypsy band playing for the diners. However, there are also many restaurants outside the towns, which are usually less expensive. Csarda – small 'folk' restaurants – can be found in villages all over Hungary and they have a cosy authentic feel.

In the summer, Hungarians enjoy spending time in 'beer gardens' – open-air restaurants often located at beauty spots. Since the boundaries have come down between East and West, fast-food establishments have found their way into Hungary, and hamburger restaurants and hot-dog stands are common.

▲ *Hungarian restaurants pride themselves on their hospitality. Traditional music is often played and there is always a good atmosphere.*

Transport

Hungary is an important route through Central Europe and four main motorways cross the country. The Hungarian road system is shaped like a star, with Budapest at its centre. This means that all major routes lead through the capital.

◀ *Nyugati (West) Station in Budapest.*

▼ *New buses and trolleybuses are being introduced in Hungary's major cities.*

Trains

Twenty per cent of Hungary's population lives in Budapest. Public transport is therefore important and trains play a large part in moving people to, from and within the city. The underground rail system has three lines, of which 'line one' is the oldest on the European mainland; the London underground came into operation only a few months earlier. Nyugati (West) Station is one of the most notable train stations in Budapest; it was designed by the French engineer Gustave Eiffel.

▶ *The siklo, or funicular railway that runs up to the castle in Budapest.*

There are other, more unusual, types of railway in Hungary. From the Chain Bridge in Budapest, a small funicular railway travels almost vertically upwards to the Royal Palace. On the other side of Buda, the Fogaskereku rack railway climbs upwards. The Children's Railway, formerly known as the Pioneer Railway, is unique. Its narrow-gauge line (11 km) runs through the woods on the hills of the Buda side of the city. Children aged 10 to 14 control the traffic and commercial services, and enjoy their responsibilities immensely.

Buses and trams

Trams, trolleybuses, and ordinary buses are other quick and reliable means of transportation. Their routes often run around the cities, but also far into the suburbs. Regular coach services to the other major cities in Hungary are also offered. When Hungary joined the European Union in 2004, a new transportation policy was introduced, and over the next ten years investements will be made in improving the public-transport systems.

Shipping

In summer it is possible to cross the Danube by boat. From Budapest you can travel to other cities by boat, such as Esztergom and Visegrád, or even to Vienna or Bratislava. Boat-trips on the Danube are also offered. The Danube and Tisza rivers are Hungary's most important waterways. Some river-vessels sail under foreign flags while others belong to the Hungarian MAHART shipping company. MAHART is the largest transportation enterprise, carrying 1.5 million passengers a year.

▼ *Ferries run day cruises down the Danube from Budapest.*

The Rhine-Main-Danube Channel, which opened in 1992, allows vessels to travel from Rotterdam Harbour as far inland as Budapest and from there to the Black Sea.

Lake Balaton is the largest lake in Central Europe and shipping traffic there is heavy. Fast catamaran ferries travel between the north and south shores of the lake. A special licence is required to sail on Lake Balaton using private motor boats.

Aviation

Malév Hungarian Airlines is Hungary's national airline carrier. The airport used to be frequented by old Russian passenger aircraft, but today these are only used as cargo planes.

Malév flies to and from various Western and Eastern European destinations, via Budapest, to the Middle East and North Africa. Direct flights are also offered to a number of cities further afield, including New York and Bangkok.

▲ *Passenger ferries carry locals and tourists between the north and south shores of Lake Balaton.*

WELCOME TO
Budapest Ferihegy Airport

◄ *Ferihegy is Hungary's only international airport. It is located 16 km outside Budapest.*

The economy

Before 1989, the Hungarian economy was made up of around 2,000 state-owned enterprises. Since the decline of Communism, however, many of these have been privatised and the economy has grown steadily.

Of all the former Warsaw Pact countries, Hungary understood the need to attract foreign interest the most. Today, the country's biggest investors are Germany and the Netherlands. The region around Budapest is profiting most from the economic growth. The eastern and north-eastern regions are lagging behind and unemployment is high in these areas.

Car manufacture

One of the first foreign companies to build factories in Hungary after 1989 was the Japanese car manufacturer Suzuki, and these cars soon became a common sight on the streets of Hungary. Today, car manufacture in the country is enhanced by the German company Audi, which has a huge plant in the city of Győr, near the border with Austria. It is one of Hungary's most important industries.

▲ *Chassis for trucks and buses are made in the Raba plant in Győr. Raba was one of the companies that was owned by the state in the communist era.*

◀ *The Audi plant in Győr. The German-owned company opened its factory in Hungary in 1994 and almost the entire range of Audi engines are now produced there.*

More and more overseas companies are investing in Hungarian businesses. Many are taking over Hungarian companies and modernising them, and productivity is being greatly increased. However, there is a negative side to this, in that improvement and modernisation have resulted in job losses in some areas.

There are other disadvantages. For example, Hungary has always been renowned for its food industry, notably sausages and salamis, but many companies have been taken over by international food conglomerates, and this has sometimes resulted in a decline in the quality of the product.

Import and export

Agriculture accounts for around 4 per cent of Hungary's economy (services cover the largest share at around 62 per cent, and industry is around 34 per cent).

Hungarian imports and exports have increased dramatically within a short space of time, and today the country's largest trading partners are other members of the European Union. Hungary lacks the extensive resources of energy and minerals that are needed for large-scale industrial development. Many mining areas are located just outside its borders. Therefore, the country has to import about half of its energy (fuel and electricity).

▲ A modern canning plant in eastern Hungary.

▼ Porcelain is made in the Zsolnay factory in Pecs.

The Kovács family is shucking corn. They are pleased with the harvest. After the revolution in 1989, many farmers were given back their land. Most of them are now smallholders (owning around 5–10 hectares of land). They mainly cultivate grain, and with family and friends they form small co-operatives to work the fields together. Everyone helps each other. Gathering the harvest is a happy event, livened up with stories and songs.

Other imports include machinery and equipment, and some foodstuffs. The main countries it imports from are Germany, Austria, Italy and Russia.

Germany is Hungary's most important export partner, although the country also exports materials to Austria, Italy, France, the USA and the UK. Machinery and equiment make up more than 50 per cent of its export products. It also exports food products and a small amount of raw materials.

Agriculture

Agricultural products include wheat, corn, sunflower seeds, potatoes, sugar beet, pigs, cattle and dairy products. During the communist regime land was owned by the state, but now most farmers have regained their land and work with family and friends in farming co-operatives.

Wine

Hungary is an important wine-producing country, and wine has been exported to other European countries since medieval times. The famous Tokaji dessert wine, for example, was the favourite drink of the French king, Louis XIV. Besides the well-known Bull's Blood of Eger, Kadarka was the favourite wine of the Imperial Court at Vienna.

Hungary exports about 30 per cent of its annual output and 40 per cent of this goes to European Union markets.

▶ *Tokaji dessert wine and 'Bull's Blood' red wine from Egri Bikaver.*

Nature

Hungarians take the protection of their natural environment seriously. Although there are environmental issues to be addressed, many laws have been introduced to maintain the country's natural beauty and to reverse some of the damage that has been done in the past.

The greater part of the country used to be covered with woods, but due to deforestation, much of this has now disappeared. In addition, the vast area of grassland called the Puszta has largely been turned into grazing land and many of the plants and animals that once flourished in this region have now disappeared or been forced to make their homes elsewhere. The species of grass growing in the Puszta is called 'needlegrass' and is under increased protection to make sure it doesn't disappear completely. This rare species of grass is nicknamed 'orphan-girl's hair'. Herdsmen used to wear a sprig of the grass in their hats, but this practice is now forbidden.

Many protected areas have been established in Hungary by local authorities to safeguard the 'original' habitat of the country's flora and fauna. These include nine national parks, 38 national landscape conservation districts, 142 national conservation areas, one natural monument (Aggtelek-Rudabánya-Szendëo) and 1,125 regional conservation districts.

▲ Hungary's amazing cave systems are among the most important protected areas in the country.

◀ A symphony orchestra gives a concert in the Aggtelek Grotto.

The Puszta

Because the soil in the vast, dry, grassy plains (steppes) in the north-east of Hungary contains high levels of salt, it is difficult for farmers to grow their crops. The land was and still is mainly used by herdsmen (often Roma), who graze their cattle and sheep there. The less-saline areas used to be covered with woodland, but these have nearly all disappeared. A scattering of swamps and small lakes can be found on the Puszta. Typical animals that can be found in this region are Hungarian grey cattle, wild horses and racka (long-wool) sheep. The heaviest flying land-bird in the world is also found there: the rare great bustard, which can weigh up to 18 kilos.

▲ The Puszta region is mainly used by shepherds and cattle-herders.

Nearly 10 per cent of Hungary's territory is protected land in the form of national parks and nature reserves. The country's largest protected area is the Hortobágy National Park, which covers the Puszta region. The area has been a nature reserve since 1962, and since 1999 has been on the UNESCO World Heritage List.

Aggtelek National Park was founded in 1985 and is located in the north of Hungary. The largest stalactite (hanging-rock formation) cave in Europe can be found there: Baradla Cave, which is 26 km long (see page 40).

▲ The rare great bustard is found on the Puszta plains.

▼ This signs warns visitors that they are entering a protected area.

◄ *Hungarian grey oxen can be found in Hungary's protected areas.*

The Danube-Dráva National Park was established in 1996. It lies, as its name suggests, on a long stretch by the Dráva and Danube Rivers, and covers nearly 50,000 hectares. Among its most famous attractions are the game reserve in the Gemenc forest in the park. Many endangered plants and animals can be found here, and much of the park has recently come under increased protection to help preserve the wildlife.

The Dráva River in particular is home to many species of fish, and there are many places in the national park where visitors can enjoy this peaceful pastime.

▼ *The Danube-Dráva National Park was established in 1996. Large parts of it are strictly protected.*

Plants

In the foothills of the Alps and in the Transdanubian Hills, oak woods can be found, occasionally alternating with coniferous trees. Due to the high levels of salt in the soil, salt-loving plants abound there. These include orache (goosefoot). In the south of the country, primeval forests can still be found – these are ancient forests that have not been affected by human activity, and are therefore well preserved. These forests consist of a mixture of deciduous and coniferous trees. Plants that grow there include hellebore (Christmas rose), Hungarian autumn crocus, and monkey orchid.

▲ *Nature and tourism go hand-in-hand in Hungary. The country's policies of natural protection mean that there are many areas of natural beauty that attract thousands of visitors every year.*

▼ *A canal in eastern Hungary, bordered by rushes.*

◀ The Hungarian grey ox is a descendant of the wild ox that used to roam the plains in ancient times.

▼ Owls are quite rare in Hungary, and are one of the protected species of bird.

Animals

A relatively large number of bird and butterfly species can be found in Hungary, mainly because agriculture is small scale and does not disturb the natural environment. Moreover, Hungarian farmers have not used pesticides on a large scale in the past. Hungary is also a country with a wide variety of landscapes, located at the crossroads of several natural migration routes.

Notable birds that live in Hungary are the corncrake, the imperial eagle, the roller, and the bee-eater. Other animal species are the viviparous lizard in Nyírség, and the 'blind lobster of Abaliget' in the Mecsek Mountains.

◀ Wild red deer are common in Hungary, and hunting of the animals is permitted at certain times of year.

▲ *The Trabant, an 'eastern-bloc' car that emits strong exhaust fumes.*

Environmental issues

The environment suffered under the communist regime, and little attention was paid to issues of pollution and damage to the natural environment; the country is still trying to redress the damage done during that time. For example, 60 to 70 per cent of sewage water from Budapest drains into the River Danube without being treated. In the rest of the country there are few sewer systems or sewage-treatment plants. Many factories discharge their sewage directly into rivers and streams.

Now that Hungary is a member of the European Union, it has to observe strict environmental rules and regulations. Since 1998, laws have been introduced to improve sewage filtering and hazardous-waste processing. By 2015, it is hoped that most villages and cities will have a sewer and a sewage-treatment plant.

▼ *Although there are now several recycling areas in Hungary, they are still not widely used. This empty collection centre is in Budapest.*

Hungary in the EU

Hungary was accepted as a full member of the European Union on 1 May 2004. This was a significant moment for the country, as it allowed Hungary to start building on the international relationships it had been cultivating since 1989, improving the economy, trade and industry, and opening up many other opportunities.

Until 1989, Hungary was part of the communist block of countries in Eastern Europe, and Russian soldiers were stationed there. Hungary's commercial ties, therefore, were for the most part restricted to other members of this economic community, such as the Soviet Union, Bulgaria, Czechoslovakia, Poland, Romania, East Germany, Mongolia, Cuba and Vietnam. Hungarian authors could only publish their works abroad and had to smuggle their manuscripts out of the country to do so. It was a difficult time for the Hungarian people.

Immediately after the fall of the communist government, Hungary opened its frontiers to the West. In 1999, the country became a member of NATO, and on 1 May 2004, Hungary joined the European Union.

▲ Women dressed in traditional Hungarian costumes cast their votes on whether or not their country should join the EU.

◀ Members of the public and media observing the Hungarian parliament at work from the visitors' gallery.

Iceland

The Countries of the European Union

Republic of Ireland	Portugal	Estonia	Finland	Austria
United Kingdom	Germany	Sweden	Greece	Latvia
Czech Republic	Denmark	Belgium	Poland	Spain
Luxembourg	Hungary	Slovakia	France	Italy
The Netherlands	Lithuania	Slovenia	Cyprus	Malta

N O R T H   S E

Republic
of
Ireland

United Kingdom

The N

Belgium

Luxem

A T L A N T I C   O C E A N

France

Switzer

Monaco

Portugal

Spain

M E D I T E R R A N E A

0   500 km

0   500 miles

Glossary

Comecon An organisation extablished in 1949 to promote the economic development of the communist countries under Soviet influence.

Communism A political system based on the principles of shared wealth and power.

Constitution A series of laws outlining the basic principles of a government or country.

Counter-Reformation The Catholic reaction to the Protestant Reformation in the sixteenth century.

Iron Curtain A theoretical boundary established after the Second World War, in which Europe was divided into the communist East and the 'free' West.

NATO North Atlantic Treaty Organization, established in 1949 to work towards security and co-operation between the member states.

Reformation The Protestant movement begun in the early sixteenth century in Europe as a reaction against corruption in the Catholic Church.

Warsaw Pact A defence organisation formed after the Second World War by communist-ruled countries in Eastern Europe.

Index

International relations

The Hungarian government supports Hungarians abroad as much as possible. For example, money is allocated for education in the Hungarian language to those living outside its borders. The neighbouring countries in which Hungarian communities exist do not always approve of this, believing that it interferes in their internal affairs.

Large Hungarian communities can be found in distant countries. The Hungarian emigration began in 1919, after the country's borders were reset. During the economic depression of the 1930s, many Hungarian children were sent abroad. In 1956, when Russian troops crushed the Hungarian Uprising, many Hungarians fled abroad.

A large community lives in Romania, and because the country has not yet joined the European Union there are fears that it will be more difficult for people to travel between the two countries than it was before. Many people in Hungary have family living across the borders in other European countries and they worry that they may not be able to see them so often.

▼ *Hungarian citizens celebrate joining the EU on the Chain Bridge in Budapest.*